Many people find a gentle touch to be comfc [...]
weighted blankets are becoming popular for helping children and adults with anxiety, sensory problems, restless legs, autism, and other disorders. Readymade ones can be quite expensive, but our instructions make it simple for even beginners to sew custom-sized blankets, lap pads, or neck wraps.

LEISURE ARTS, INC. • Maumelle, Arkansas

Why a Weighted Blanket?

A weighted blanket molds to your body like a warm hug. Doctors and therapists believe that the pressure helps relax the nervous system and causes the brain to release neurotransmitters like serotonin and dopamine that improve moods and induce a calming effect. This helps many people relax naturally.

Weighted blankets are often used by people with autism, Asperger's syndrome, restless leg syndrome, chronic pain, anxiety, stress, sensory processing disorders, and many other conditions. Many people use them just because they believe the weight of the blanket helps them sleep better.

Consult your doctor or occupational therapist regarding using a weighted blanket - the correct size, the correct weight, and the duration for use. Do not use a weighted blanket if you have respiratory, circulatory, or temperature regulation problems, or post surgery. We do not recommend weighted blankets for children younger than 6 years of age. Never leave a small child unattended when using a weighted blanket. Make sure the child is strong enough to push the blanket off, if necessary.

Supplies

Fabrics

For most of our blanket tops we used quilt weight 100% cotton fabrics, but we also used some beautiful wool flannels. For the backing, quilt weight 100% cotton fabric or 100% cotton flannel is suitable but a plush "sensory" fabric, such as, fleece, minky, or chenille is also very desirable. Plush fabrics are available in solids, prints, embossed, and double-sided.

Plastic Poly Pellets

Use safe, non-toxic hypo-allergenic polypropylene pellets for weighting your blanket. They are machine washable and dryable.

Digital Food Scale

For accuracy, use a digital food scale to weigh the pellets to put in each pouch.

Sewing Machine Needles

Use a size 10 (70) needle for piecing the blocks. Use a size 14 (90) denim needle for sewing the blanket top and backing together. Denim needles have a sharp point and a strong shaft that can stitch through many layers without breaking. Try to avoid hitting the poly pellets as you sew.

Thread

When sewing quilt weight 100% cotton fabrics for the blanket top, use all-purpose sewing thread in both the needle and the bobbin. All-purpose thread is also suitable for sewing the blanket top to a quilt weight 100% cotton backing. If using a plush fabric for the backing, use 100% polyester thread in both the needle and the bobbin.

Walking Foot or Even Feed Foot

Use a walking foot on your machine when sewing the blanket top to the backing. This foot will help eliminate puckering and helps feed the fabric layers together at the same time.

Wrapping Paper Tube

Use a wrapping paper tube to help feed the pellets into the channels of the blanket. A piece of PVC pipe or a vacuum cleaner extension tube can also be used.

Kitchen Funnel

You may find it helpful to tape a kitchen funnel to the end of the wrapping paper tube. This will help reduce spilling.

Determining the Blanket Size

A weighted blanket can be used by laying it across the lap or torso, wrapping it around the shoulders, covering just the legs, or covering the entire body for sleeping. If using the weighted blanket for sleeping, the blanket should fit the body, not the bed. It should be big enough to cover the body from the tip of the chin to just past the toes. But children grow quickly; you may choose to allow a little extra length for growing room.

Choose the size depending on the intended use and the height of the user.

Preparing the Fabrics

We recommend that all fabrics be washed and dried before cutting. If fabrics are not pre-washed, washing the finished blanket may cause shrinkage. Bright and dark colors, which may run, should always be washed before cutting. Cotton fabrics should be washed using warm water and tumble dried on low. Cotton fabrics need to be pressed after washing. Plush fabrics should be washed using cold water and tumble dried on low or hung to dry. Plush fabrics **should not** be pressed as they can melt when exposed to the high heat of the iron. If pressing is necessary, use low temperature and a press cloth. After washing and drying fabric, fold lengthwise with wrong sides together and matching selvages for cutting.

Determining the Blanket Weight

Consult your healthcare professional to determine the best weight blanket to make. For children and young teens, we recommend the pellets in your blanket weigh 10% of the body weight plus 1 pound. For older teens and adults this formula may become very heavy. These blankets should be 5%-10% of your body weight but should not exceed 20 pounds.

Convert the desired weight in pounds to ounces by multiplying the weight by 16 oz. Divide the total ounces by the number of pouches given in the project instructions. Use the scale to determine the amount of pellets. Place this amount in each pouch.

For example:
A 50 lb. child would require 6 pounds of pellets
(50 lb. x 10% + 1 lb. = 6 lbs.)

Multiply the weight by 16 oz. (6 lb. x 16 oz. = 96 oz.)

Divide the total ounces by the number of pouches stated in the project instructions for the size blanket you are making. (96 oz. ÷ 117 pouches = 0.82 oz. per pouch.) Place the determined number of ounces in each pouch.

Tip:

To speed up the process, find a container to scoop and measure the pellets for each pouch. This could be a measuring cup or a foam cup on which you have marked a line. On our blankets, very often the amount was nearest a 1/4 cup measuring cup.

Rotary Cutting

While a rotary cutter and ruler can be used to cut the blanket backing, these instructions primarily pertain to cutting the pieces for the blocks.

- Place fabric on work surface with fold closest to you.
- Cut all strips from the selvage-to-selvage width of the fabric unless otherwise indicated in project instructions.
- Square left edge of fabric using rotary cutter and rulers (**Figs. 1-2**).
- To cut each strip required for a project, place ruler over cut edge of fabric, aligning desired marking on ruler with cut edge; make cut (**Fig. 3**).
- If cutting several strips from a single piece of fabric, it is important to make sure that cuts remain at a perfect right angle to the fold; square fabric as needed.

Fig. 1

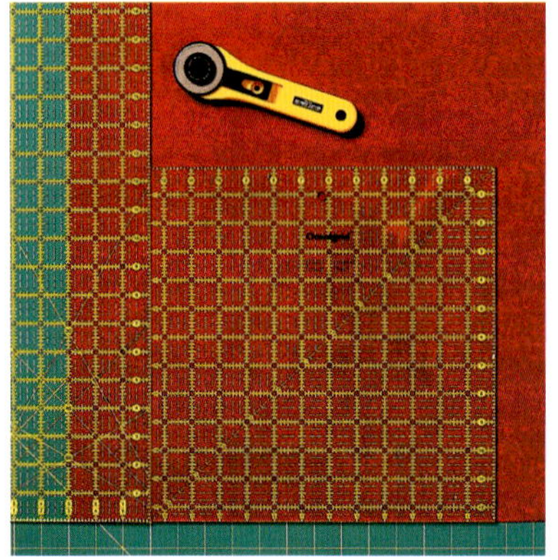

Fig. 2

Fig. 3

Piecing the Blocks

Precise cutting, followed by accurate piecing, will ensure that all pieces of blanket top fit together well.

- Use a size 10 (70) sewing machine needle for piecing the blocks.
- For most sewing, set sewing machine stitch length for approximately 11 stitches per inch. When sewing fleece or Minky, set sewing machine stitch length for approximately 8-10 stitches per inch.
- Use all-purpose sewing thread (not quilting thread) in needle and in bobbin.
- An accurate 1/4" seam allowance is essential. Presser feet that are 1/4" wide are available for most sewing machines.
- When piecing, always place pieces right sides together and match raw edges; pin if necessary.
- Chain piecing saves time and will usually result in more accurate piecing.
- Trim away points of seam allowances that extend beyond edges of sewn pieces.
- When sewing fleece or Minky, loosen the presser foot pressure to reduce shifting.

Sewing Across Seam Intersections

When sewing across intersection of two seams, place pieces right sides together and match seams exactly, making sure seam allowances are pressed in opposite directions **(Fig. 4)**.

Fig. 4

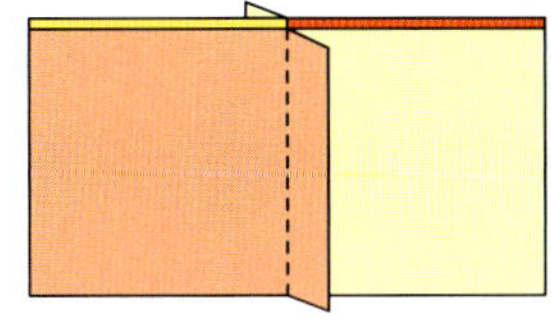

Sewing Sharp Points

To ensure sharp points when joining triangular or diagonal pieces, stitch across the center of the "X" (shown in pink) formed on wrong side by previous seams **(Fig. 5)**.

Fig. 5

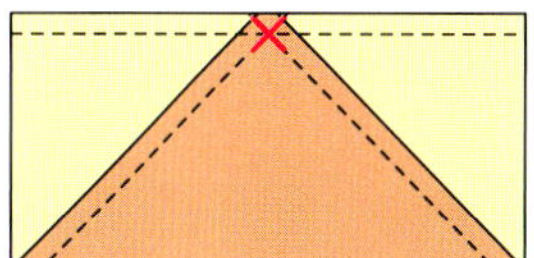

Pressing

- Use steam iron set on "Cotton" when pressing cotton fabrics. Because plush fabrics can melt when exposed to high heat, do not use an iron. Finger press the fabric whenever possible. If pressing is necessary, use low temperature and a press cloth.
- When piecing the blanket top, press after sewing each seam. Seam allowances are almost always pressed to one side, usually toward the darker fabric. However, to reduce bulk it may occasionally be necessary to press seam allowances toward the lighter fabric or even to press them open. To prevent the dark fabric seam allowance from showing through light fabric, trim darker seam allowance slightly narrower than lighter seam allowance.

Marking Stitching Lines

Stitching lines for vertical and horizontal channels may be marked using fabric marking pencils, chalk markers, or water- or air-soluble pens.

Caution: Pressing may permanently set some marks. Test different markers on scrap fabric to find one that marks clearly and can be thoroughly removed.

Assembling The Blanket

Attach a walking foot to your sewing machine. Backstitch at beginning and end of stitching and use 1/4" seam allowances throughout.

1. Follow project instructions to assemble Blanket Top.

2. If the backing for the blanket is 40" wide or more, two lengths will need to be pieced together for the backing. Cut the fabric into two equal lengths. Match right sides and raw edges and sew lengths together. Trim backing to size given in project instructions.

3. Press 1 short edge of Blanket Top and **backing** 1/4" to wrong side.

4. Matching right sides and pressed edges, sew Blanket Top to backing along long edges and unpressed short edge **(Fig. 6)**. Clip corners, turn right side out, and press. *(**Note:** If using a plush fabric backing, sew with the plush fabric on the bottom and the cotton fabrics on the top. Sometimes the plush fabric will stretch or shift. To help prevent this, pin layers together every 1" and lengthen your stitch length. It may also be helpful to reduce the presser foot pressure.)*

Fig. 6

5. The project instructions will tell you where to mark the vertical and horizontal channels. The placement of the vertical and horizontal channels will depend on the size of the blanket, the number of blocks, and the number of seams in the blocks. Often the stitching line will be on a seamline; this should be done directly on the seamline or just to the side of the seamline opposite the seam allowances. This stitching line does not have to be marked. Refer to **Fig. 7** and follow the project instructions to mark and stitch the vertical channels.

Fig. 7

6. Follow project instructions to mark the horizontal channels on the blanket top.

7. Tape the kitchen funnel to the end of the wrapping paper tube. Place the tube in the first channel on one side. Pour the determined amount of pellets in the tube. Let the pellets fall all the way to the bottom of the channel. Work side to side to fill each channel. Keeping the pellets out of the way, stitch a horizontal channel to form the first row of pouches **(Fig. 8)**.

Fig. 8

8. Pour pellets in each vertical channel again. Let them fall all the way to the bottom. Stitch a horizontal channel to form the next row of pouches.

9. Continue filling and sewing horizontal channels until all the pouches are filled **(Fig. 9)**.

10. After filling the final pouches, topstitch the pressed edges closed.

Fig. 9

Laundering

Your blanket can be machine washed and dried depending on the capacity of your washer and dryer.

Tip: You may find it helpful to slide a pencil across the fabric and push the pellets to the bottom of the pouches as you sew. You can also insert a row of pins to hold the pellets at the bottom.

Super Simple

Youth Small, Finished Size:
36" x 48" (91 cm x 122 cm)
For information on other blanket sizes, refer to the table on page 9.

SHOPPING LIST

Yardage is based on 43"/44" (109 cm/112 cm) wide fabric with a usable width of 40" (102 cm).

- ☐ 1⁵/₈ yds (1.5 m) of fabric for blanket top
- ☐ 1⁵/₈ yds (1.5 m) of fabric for backing
- ☐ plastic poly pellets (see **Step 1**, page 9)
- ☐ walking foot
- ☐ size 14 (90) denim sewing machine needle
- ☐ wrapping paper tube
- ☐ kitchen funnel
- ☐ measuring cup
- ☐ water-soluble fabric marking pen

Cutting The Pieces

All measurements include 1/4" seam allowances.

From fabric for blanket top:

- Cut **blanket top** 36 1/2" x 48 1/2".

From fabric for backing:

- Cut **backing** 36 1/2" x 48 1/2".

Assembling The Blanket

Read pages 2-7, before beginning your blanket. Use 1/4" seam allowances throughout.

1. Refer to **Determining the Blanket Weight**, page 3, to determine the quantity of pellets needed for the blanket and how much to place in each pouch. This blanket has 108 pouches.

2. *Refer to **Assembling the Blanket**, pages 6-7, to assemble, fill, and close the blanket.* After sewing blanket top to backing, mark the vertical and horizontal stitching lines (shown in red) 4" apart on the blanket top **(Fig. 1)**. Stitch vertically along each marked line to make 9 vertical channels. Place determined amount of pellets in each channel. Stitch horizontally along each marked line to make 12 horizontal channels. Close the blanket.

The following table provides the information necessary to make your blanket in other sizes.

	Youth Medium	Youth Large	Adult Small	Adult Medium	Adult Large	Adult X-Large
Finished Size	36" x 52"	36" x 56"	40" x 60"	44" x 64"	48" x 68"	52" x 72"
Fabric Requirements	1 5/8 yds (1.5 m) of fabric for blanket top 1 5/8 yds (1.5 m) of fabric for backing	1 3/4 yds (1.6 m) of fabric for blanket top 1 3/4 yds (1.6 m) of fabric for backing	1 7/8 yds (1.7 m) of fabric for blanket top 1 7/8 yds (1.7 m) of fabric for backing	3 7/8 yds (3.5 m) of fabric for blanket top 3 7/8 yds (3.5 m) of fabric for backing	4 1/8 yds (3.8 m) of fabric for blanket top 4 1/8 yds (3.8 m) of fabric for backing	4 3/8 yds (4 m) of fabric for blanket top 4 3/8 yds (4 m) of fabric for backing
Channel Grid	9 x 13	9 x 14	10 x 15	11 x 16	12 x 17	13 x 18
Pellet Pouches	117	126	150	176	204	234
Blanket Top Cut Size	36 1/2" x 52 1/2"	36 1/2" x 56 1/2"	40 1/2" x 60 1/2"	44 1/2" x 64 1/2", pieced as necessary	48 1/2" x 68 1/2", pieced as necessary	52 1/2" x 72 1/2", pieced as necessary
Backing Cut Size	36 1/2" x 52 1/2"	36 1/2" x 56 1/2"	40 1/2" x 60 1/2"	44 1/2" x 64 1/2", pieced as necessary	48 1/2" x 68 1/2", pieced as necessary	52 1/2" x 72 1/2", pieced as necessary

Teal Squares

Youth Medium/Adult Small,
Finished Size: 38" x 57" (97 cm x 145 cm)
Finished Block Size: $9^1/_2$" x $9^1/_2$" (24 cm x 24 cm)
For information on other blanket sizes, refer to the table on page 11.

SHOPPING LIST

Yardage is based on 43"/44" (109 cm/112 cm) wide fabric with a usable width of 40" (102 cm). Layer Cakes are approximately 10" x 10" (25 cm x 25 cm).

- ☐ 1 Layer Cake or $^5/_8$ yd (57 cm) **each** of four assorted prints
- ☐ $1^3/_4$ yds (1.6 m) of fabric for backing
- ☐ plastic poly pellets (see **Step 3**, page 11)
- ☐ walking foot
- ☐ size 10 (70) sewing machine needle and size 14 (90) denim sewing machine needle
- ☐ wrapping paper tube
- ☐ kitchen funnel
- ☐ measuring cup
- ☐ water-soluble fabric marking pen

Assembling The Blanket

Read pages 2-7 before beginning your blanket. Use 1/4" seam allowances throughout.

1. Sew 4 **squares** together to make a Row. Make 6 Rows. Press seam allowances in one direction.

2. Alternating direction of seam allowances, sew Rows together to make the **Blanket Top**.

3. Refer to **Determining the Blanket Weight**, page 3, to determine the quantity of pellets needed for the blanket and how much to place in each pouch. This blanket has 96 pouches.

4. *Refer to **Assembling the Blanket**, pages 6-7, to assemble, fill, and close the blanket.* After sewing blanket top to backing, mark the vertical and horizontal stitching lines (shown in red) across each square **(Fig. 1)**. Stitch vertically between each block on the seamline and across the squares vertically where marked to make 8 vertical channels. Place determined amount of pellets in each channel. Stitch horizontally between each block on the seamline and across the squares horizontally where marked to make 12 horizontal channels. Close the blanket.

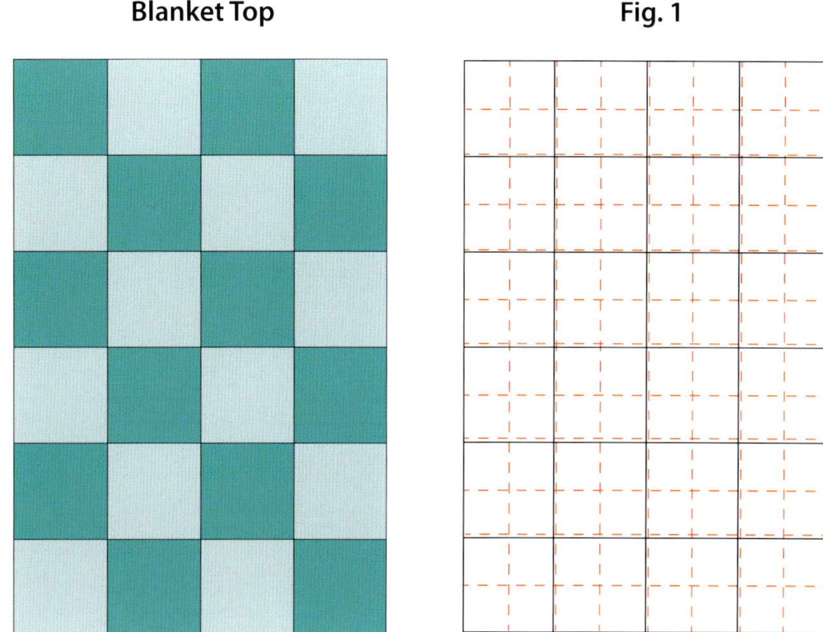
Blanket Top **Fig. 1**

The following table provides the information necessary to make your blanket in other sizes.

	Youth Small	Youth Large	Adult Medium	Adult Large	Adult X-Large
Finished Size	38" x 47 1/2"	38" x 66 1/2"	47 1/2" x 66 1/2"	47 1/2" x 76"	57" x 76"
Fabric Requirements	1 Layer Cake **or** 5/8 yd (57 cm) **each** of four assorted prints 1 1/2 yds (1.4 m) of fabric for backing	1 Layer Cake **or** 5/8 yd (57 cm) **each** of four assorted prints 2 yds (1.8 m) of fabric for backing	1 Layer Cake **or** 1 yd (91 cm) **each** of four assorted prints 4 yds (3.7 m) of fabric for backing	1 Layer Cake **or** 1 yd (91 cm) **each** of four assorted prints 4 1/2 yds (4.1 m) of fabric for backing	2 Layer Cakes **or** 1 yd (91 cm) **each** of four assorted prints 4 1/2 yds (4.1 m) of fabric for backing
Number of Blocks	20	28	35	40	48
Block Set	4 x 5	4 x 7	5 x 7	5 x 8	6 x 8
Pellet Pouches	80	112	140	160	192
Each of Four Assorted Prints	5 **squares** 10" x 10"	7 **squares** 10" x 10"	9 **squares** 10" x 10"; you will use 35	10 **squares** 10" x 10"	12 **squares** 10" x 10"
Backing Cut Size	38 1/2" x 48"	38 1/2" x 67"	48" x 67", pieced as necessary	48" x 76 1/2", pieced as necessary	57 1/2" x 76 1/2", pieced as necessary

Charm Squares

Youth Small, Finished Size: 36" x 45" (91 cm x 114 cm)
Finished Block Size: $4^1/_2$" x $4^1/_2$" (11 cm x 11 cm)
For information on other blanket sizes, refer to the table on page 13.

SHOPPING LIST

Yardage is based on 43"/44" (109 cm/112 cm) wide fabric with a usable width of 40" (102 cm). Charm squares are approximately 5" x 5" (13 cm x 13 cm).

- ☐ 80 assorted charm squares **or** 5" x 5" (13 cm x 13 cm) squares
- ☐ $1^3/_8$ yds (1.3 m) of fabric for backing
- ☐ plastic poly pellets (see **Step 3**, page 13)
- ☐ size 10 (70) sewing machine needle and size 14 (90) denim sewing machine needle
- ☐ walking foot
- ☐ wrapping paper tube
- ☐ kitchen funnel
- ☐ measuring cup

Cutting The Pieces

All measurements include 1/4" seam allowances.

From fabric for backing:

- Cut **backing** 36 1/2" x 45 1/2".

Assembling The Blanket

Read pages 2-7 before beginning your blanket. Use 1/4" seam allowances throughout.

1. Sew 8 squares together to make a **Row**. Make 10 Rows. Press seam allowances in alternating directions.

Row

2. Sew Rows together to make **Blanket Top**. Press all seam allowances toward bottom.

3. Refer to **Determining the Blanket Weight**, page 3, to determine the quantity of pellets needed for the blanket and how much to place in each pouch. This blanket has 80 pouches.

4. *Refer to **Assembling the Blanket**, pages 6-7, to assemble, fill, and close the blanket.* After sewing blanket top to backing, stitch along each vertical seamline (shown in red) to make 8 vertical channels **(Fig. 1)**. Place determined amount of pellets in each channel. Stitch horizontally along each horizontal seamline (shown in red) to make 12 horizontal channels. Close the blanket.

Fig. 1

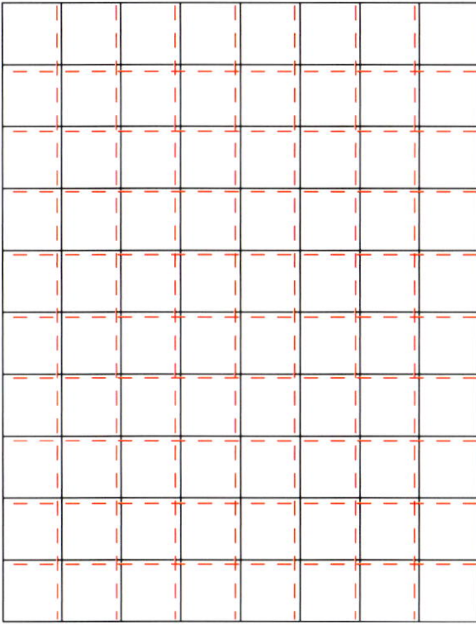

Blanket Top

The following table provides the information necessary to make your blanket in other sizes.

	Youth Medium or Adult Small	Youth Large or Adult Medium	Adult Large	Adult X-Large
Finished Size	36" x 54"	36" x 63"	45" x 72"	54" x 72"
Fabric Requirements	3 Charm Packs **or** 96 assorted 5" x 5" (13 cm x 13 cm) squares 1 3/4 yds (1.6 m) of fabric for backing	3 Charm Packs **or** 112 assorted 5" x 5" (13 cm x 13 cm) squares 2 yds (1.8 m) of fabric for backing	4 Charm Packs **or** 160 assorted 5" x 5" (13 cm x 13 cm) squares 4 3/8 yds (4 m) of fabric for backing	5 Charm Packs **or** 192 assorted 5" x 5" (13 cm x 13 cm) squares 4 3/8 yds (4 m) of fabric for backing
Square Set	8 x 12	8 x 14	10 x 16	12 x 16
Pellet Pouches	96	112	160	192
Backing Cut Size	36 1/2" x 54 1/2"	36 1/2" x 63 1/2"	45 1/2" x 72 1/2", pieced as necessary	54 1/2" x 72 1/2", pieced as necessary

Plaid Flannels

Adult Extra-Large, Finished Size: 50" x 80" (127 cm x 203 cm)
Finished Block Size: 10" x 10" (25 cm x 25 cm)
For information on other blanket sizes, refer to the table on page 17.

SHOPPING LIST

Yardage is based on 43"/44" (109 cm/112 cm) wide fabric with a usable width of 40" (102 cm). Fat quarters are approximately 22" x 18" (56 cm x 46 cm.)

- ☐ 20 fat quarters of assorted light and dark plaid flannel fabrics for blocks
- ☐ 4 3/4 yds (4.3 m) of fabric for backing
- ☐ plastic poly pellets (see **Step 8**, page 17)
- ☐ walking foot
- ☐ size 10 (70) sewing machine needle and size 14 (90) denim sewing machine needle
- ☐ wrapping paper tube
- ☐ kitchen funnel
- ☐ measuring cup
- ☐ water-soluble fabric marking pen

Cutting The Pieces

*Follow **Rotary Cutting**, page 4, to cut fabric. Refer to **Cutting Diagram** to cut each fat quarter.*

From each fat quarter:

- Cut 1 **large square** 10 1/2" x 10 1/2".
- Cut 4 **small squares** 5 1/2" x 5 1/2".

Cutting Diagram

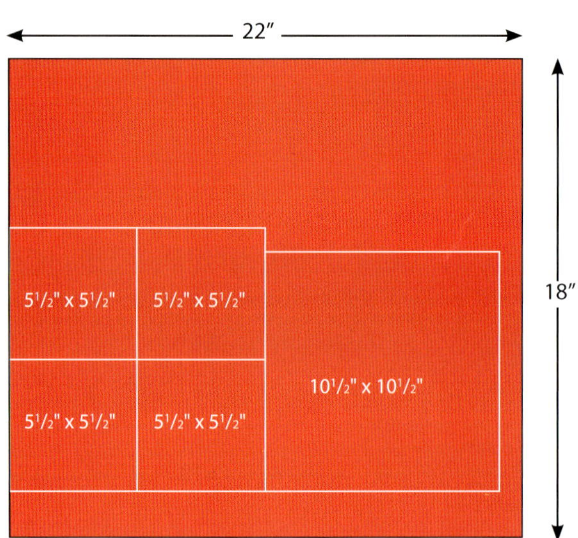

From fabric for backing:

- Cut 2 **backing** lengths 40 1/2" x 80 1/2".

Assembling The Blanket

Read pages 2-7 before beginning your blanket. Use ¼" seam allowances throughout.

1. Sew 1 assorted dark **small square** and 1 assorted light **small square** together to make a **Unit 1**. Press the seam allowances toward the darker fabric. Make 2 Unit 1's.

Unit 1 (make 2)

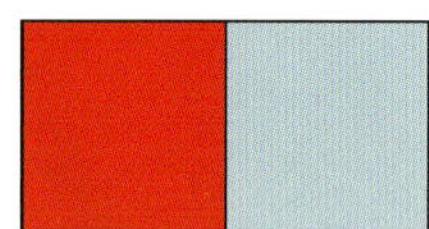

2. Sew 2 Unit 1's together to make a **4-Patch Block**. Remove a few stitches in the previously sewn seam allowances to allow seam allowances in center to press in opposite directions like a pinwheel **(Fig.1)**.

4-Patch Block

Fig. 1

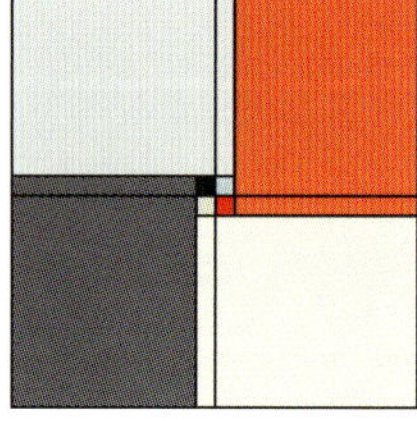

3. Repeat Steps 1-2 to make a total of 20 4-Patch Blocks.

4. Sew 3 4-Patch Blocks and 2 **large squares** together to make **Row A**. Make 4 Row A's. Press seam allowances in one direction.

Row A (make 4)

5. Sew 3 large squares and 2 4-Patch Blocks together to make **Row B**. Make 4 Row B's. Press seam allowances in the opposite direction.

Row B (make 4)

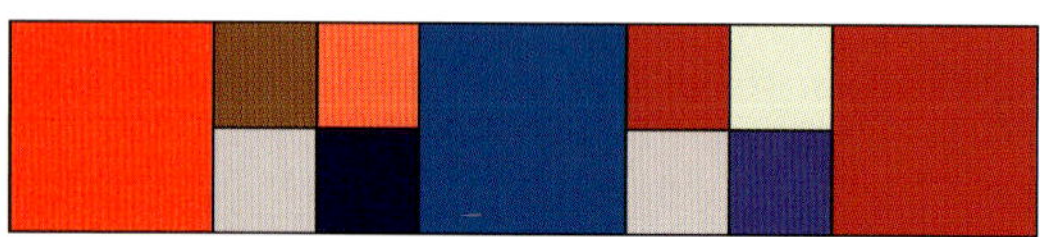

6. Alternating direction of seam allowances, sew Rows together to make blanket top. Press seam allowances toward the bottom of the blanket top.

Blanket Top

7. Matching long edges, sew **backing** lengths together; press seam allowances open. Trim backing to 50$^1/_2$" x 80$^1/_2$".

8. Refer to **Determining the Blanket Weight**, page 3, to determine the quantity of pellets needed for the blanket and how much to place in each pouch. This blanket has 160 pouches.

9. *Refer to **Assembling the Blanket**, pages 6-7, to assemble, fill, and close the blanket.* After sewing blanket top to backing, mark a line through the center of each large square (shown in red) both vertically and horizontally **(Fig. 2)**. Stitch vertically between each block, along each vertical seam of each Block, and across the large squares vertically where marked to make 10 vertical channels. Place determined amount of pellets in each channel. Stitch horizontally between each block, along each horizontal seam of each Block, and across the large squares horizontally where marked as you fill the channels to make 16 horizontal channels. Close the blanket.

Fig. 2

The following table provides the information necessary to make your blanket in other sizes.

	Youth Small	Youth Medium or Adult Small	Youth Large or Adult Medium	Adult Large
Finished Size	40" x 40"	40" x 50"	40" x 60"	50" x 70"
Fabric Requirements	8 assorted plaid flannel fat quarters 1$^3/_8$ yds (1.3 m) of fabric for backing	10 assorted plaid flannel fat quarters 1$^5/_8$ yds (1.5 m) of fabric for backing	12 assorted plaid flannel fat quarters 1$^7/_8$ yds (1.7 m) of fabric for backing	18 assorted plaid flannel fat quarters 4$^1/_4$ yds (3.9 m) of fabric for backing
Number of Blocks	16	20	24	35
Block Set	4 x 4	4 x 5	4 x 6	5 x 7
Pellet Pouches	64	80	96	140
Each Fat Quarter	**1 large square** 10$^1/_2$" x 10$^1/_2$" **4 small squares** 5$^1/_2$" x 5$^1/_2$"	**1 large square** 10$^1/_2$" x 10$^1/_2$" **4 small squares** 5$^1/_2$" x 5$^1/_2$"	**1 large square** 10$^1/_2$" x 10$^1/_2$" **4 small squares** 5$^1/_2$" x 5$^1/_2$"	**1 large square** 10$^1/_2$" x 10$^1/_2$" **4 small squares** 5$^1/_2$" x 5$^1/_2$"
Backing Cut Size	40$^1/_2$" x 40$^1/_2$"	40$^1/_2$" x 50$^1/_2$"	40$^1/_2$" x 60$^1/_2$"	50$^1/_2$" x 70$^1/_2$", pieced as necessary

Rail Fence

Adult Large, Finished Size: 42" x 72" (107 cm x 183 cm)
Finished Block Size: 6" x 6" (15 cm x 15 cm)
For information on other blanket sizes, refer to the table on page 20.

SHOPPING LIST

Yardage is based on 43"/44" (109 cm/112 cm) wide fabric with a usable width of 40" (102 cm). Jelly Rolls are 2$^{1}/_{2}$" (6.35 cm) wide x approximately 40" (102 cm).

- ☐ 2 Jelly Rolls or assorted 2$^{1}/_{2}$" (6.35 cm) wide strips totalling approximately 49 yds (45 m)
- ☐ 4$^{3}/_{8}$ yds (4 m) of fabric for backing
- ☐ plastic poly pellets (see **Step 5**, page 20)
- ☐ size 10 (70) sewing machine needle and size 14 (90) denim sewing machine needle
- ☐ walking foot
- ☐ wrapping paper tube
- ☐ kitchen funnel
- ☐ measuring cup

Cutting The Pieces

*Follow **Rotary Cutting**, page 4, to cut fabric. All measurements include $^{1}/_{4}$" seam allowances.*

From Jelly Roll strips:

- Cut 252 assorted **strips** 2$^{1}/_{2}$" x 7".

From fabric for backing:

- Cut 2 **backing** lengths 40" x 72$^{1}/_{2}$".

Assembling The Blanket

Read pages 2-7 before beginning your blanket. Use $^{1}/_{4}$" seam allowances throughout.

1. Matching long edges, sew 3 assorted **strips** together to make a **Block**. Press seam allowances to one side. Trim Block to 6$^{1}/_{2}$" x 6$^{1}/_{2}$". Make 84 Blocks.

Block

2. Alternating direction of Blocks, sew 7 Blocks together to make a Row. Make 12 Rows. Press seam allowances in one direction.

3. Alternating direction of seam allowances, sew Rows together to make **Blanket Top**. Press seam allowances toward the bottom.

4. Matching right sides and long raw edges, sew backing lengths together. Press seam allowances open. Trim backing to 42$^1/_2$" x 72$^1/_2$".

5. Refer to **Determining the Blanket Weight**, page 3, to determine the quantity of pellets needed for the blanket and how much to place in each pouch. This blanket has 84 pouches.

Blanket Top

The following table provides the information necessary to make your blanket in other sizes.

	Youth Small	Youth Medium or Adult Small	Youth Large or Adult Medium	Adult X-Large
Finished Size	36" x 48"	36" x 54"	36" x 60"	54" x 72"
Fabric Requirements	1 Jelly Roll or assorted 2$^1/_2$" (6.35 cm) wide strips totalling approximately 28 yds (26 m) 1$^1/_2$ yds (1.4 m) of fabric for backing	1 Jelly Roll or assorted 2$^1/_2$" (6.35 cm) wide strips totalling approximately 31$^1/_2$ yds (29 m) 1$^3/_4$ yds (1.6 m) of fabric for backing	1 Jelly Roll or assorted 2$^1/_2$" (6.35 cm) wide strips totalling approximately 35 yds (32 m) 1$^7/_8$ yds (1.7 m) of fabric for backing	2 Jelly Rolls or assorted 2$^1/_2$" (6.35 cm) wide strips totalling approximately 63 yds (58 m) 4$^3/_8$ yds (4 m) of fabric for backing
Number of Blocks	48	54	60	108
Block Set	6 x 8	6 x 9	6 x 10	9 x 12
Pellet Pouches	48	54	60	108
Jelly Roll Strips	144 **strips** 2$^1/_2$" x 7"	162 **strips** 2$^1/_2$" x 7"	180 **strips** 2$^1/_2$" x 7"	324 **strips** 2$^1/_2$" x 7"
Backing Cut Size	36$^1/_2$" x 48$^1/_2$"	36$^1/_2$" x 54$^1/_2$"	36$^1/_2$" x 60$^1/_2$"	54$^1/_2$" x 72$^1/_2$", pieced as necessary

6. *Refer to **Assembling the Blanket**, pages 6-7, to assemble, fill, and close the blanket.* Stitch vertically between each block (shown in red) to make 7 vertical channels **(Fig. 1)**. Place determined amount of pellets in each channel. Stitch horizontally between each Block as you fill the channels to make 12 horizontal channels. Close the blanket.

Fig. 1

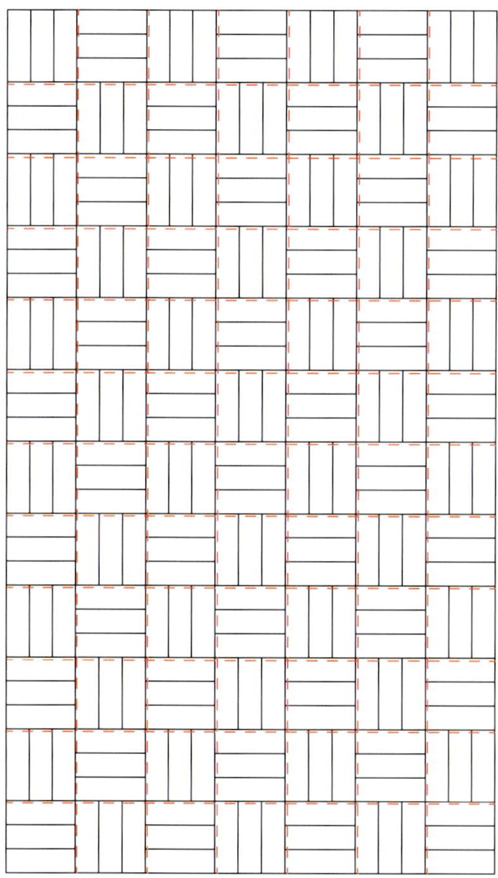

Soccer Balls

Youth Large/Adult Medium, Finished Size: 40" x 60" (102 cm x 152 cm)
Finished Block Size: 10" x 10" (25 cm x 25 cm)
For information on other blanket sizes, refer to the table on page 25.

SHOPPING LIST

Yardage is based on 43"/44" (109 cm/112 cm) wide fabric with a usable width of 40" (102 cm).

- ☐ $1^1/_4$ yds (1.1 m) of novelty print fabric for blocks
- ☐ $^3/_4$ yd (69 cm) of green solid fabric for blocks
- ☐ $^3/_4$ yd (69 cm) of blue solid fabric for blocks
- ☐ $1^7/_8$ yds (1.7 m) of fabric for backing
- ☐ plastic poly pellets (see **Step 5**, page 24)
- ☐ size 10 (70) sewing machine needle and size 14 (90) denim sewing machine needle
- ☐ walking foot
- ☐ wrapping paper tube
- ☐ kitchen funnel
- ☐ measuring cup
- ☐ water-soluble fabric marking pen

Cutting The Pieces

*Follow **Rotary Cutting**, page 4, to cut fabric. Cut all strips from the selvage-to-selvage width of the fabric. All measurements include $^1/_4$" seam allowances.*

From novelty print fabric:

- Cut 5 strips $7^1/_2$" wide. From these strips, cut 24 **center squares** $7^1/_2$" x $7^1/_2$".

From green solid fabric:

- Cut 4 strips 6" wide. From these strips, cut 24 squares 6" x 6". Cut each square once diagonally to make a total of 48 **triangles**.

From blue solid fabric:

- Cut 4 strips 6" wide. From these strips, cut 24 squares 6" x 6". Cut each square once diagonally to make a total of 48 **triangles**.

From backing fabric:

- Cut **back** $40^1/_2$" x $60^1/_2$".

Assembling The Blanket

Read pages 2-7 before beginning your blanket. Use 1/4" seam allowances throughout.

1. Sew 2 blue **triangles** to opposite sides of 1 **center square**. Press seam allowances toward center square.

2. Sew 2 green **triangles** to remaining sides of 1 center square to make 1 **Block**. Press seam allowances toward center square. Trim each block to 10 1/2" x 10 1/2".

Block (make 24)

3. Sew 4 Blocks together to make a **Row**. Make 6 Rows. Press seam allowances in one direction.
4. Alternating direction of seam allowances, sew Rows together to make **Blanket Top**. Press seam allowances toward the bottom of the blanket top.
5. Refer to **Determining the Blanket Weight**, page 3, to determine the quantity of pellets needed for the blanket and how much to place in each pouch. This blanket has 96 pouches.

6. *Refer to **Assembling the Blanket**, pages 6-7, to assemble, fill, and close the blanket.* After sewing blanket top to backing, mark the vertical and horizontal stitching lines (shown in red) through the center of each Block on the blanket top **(Fig. 1)**. Stitch vertically between each Block and across the Blocks vertically where marked to make 8 vertical channels. Place determined amount of pellets in each channel. Stitch horizontally between each Block and across the Blocks horizontally where marked as you fill to make 12 horizontal channels. Close the blanket.

Blanket Top

Fig. 1

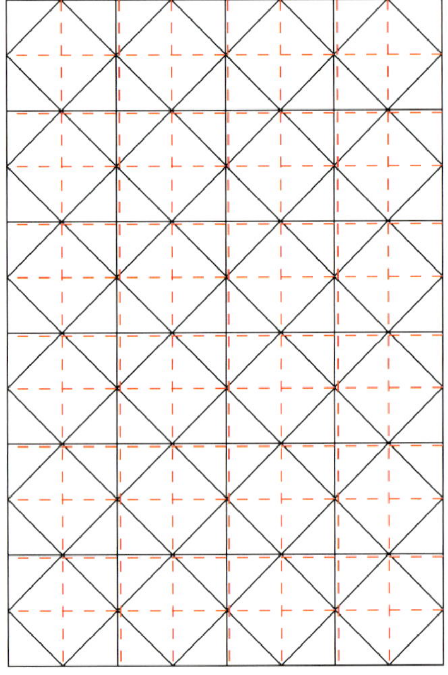

The following table provides the information necessary to make your blanket in other sizes.

	Youth Small	**Youth Medium or Adult Small**	**Adult Large**	**Adult X-Large**
Finished Size	40" x 40"	40" x 50"	40" x 70"	50" x 70"
Fabric Requirements	1 yd (91 cm) of novelty print fabric $^5/_8$ yd (57 cm) of green solid fabric $^5/_8$ yd (57 cm) of blue solid fabric $1^1/_4$ yds (1.1 m) of fabric for backing	1 yd (91 cm) of novelty print fabric $^3/_4$ yd (69 cm) of green solid fabric $^3/_4$ yd (69 cm) of blue solid fabric $1^5/_8$ yds (1.5 m) of fabric for backing	$1^3/_8$ yds (1.3 m) of novelty print fabric 1 yd (91 cm) of green solid fabric 1 yd (91 cm) of blue solid fabric $2^1/_8$ yds (1.9 m) of fabric for backing	$1^5/_8$ yds (1.5 m) of novelty print fabric $1^1/_8$ yds (1 m) of green solid fabric $1^1/_8$ yds (1 m) of blue solid fabric $4^1/_4$ yds (3.9 m) of fabric for backing
Number of Blocks	16	20	28	35
Block Set	4 x 4	4 x 5	4 x 7	5 x 7
Pellet Pouches	64	80	112	140
Novelty Print Fabric	16 **center squares** $7^1/_2$" x $7^1/_2$"	20 **center squares** $7^1/_2$" x $7^1/_2$"	28 **center squares** $7^1/_2$" x $7^1/_2$"	35 **center squares** $7^1/_2$" x $7^1/_2$"
Green Solid Fabric	Cut 16 squares 6" x 6". Cut once diagonally to make 32 **triangles.**	Cut 20 squares 6" x 6". Cut once diagonally to make 40 **triangles.**	Cut 28 squares 6" x 6". Cut once diagonally to make 56 **triangles.**	Cut 35 squares 6" x 6". Cut once diagonally to make 70 **triangles.**
Blue Solid Fabric	Cut 16 squares 6" x 6". Cut once diagonally to make 32 **triangles.**	Cut 20 squares 6" x 6". Cut once diagonally to make 40 **triangles.**	Cut 28 squares 6" x 6". Cut once diagonally to make 56 **triangles.**	Cut 35 squares 6" x 6". Cut once diagonally to make 70 **triangles.**
Backing Cut Size	$40^1/_2$" x $40^1/_2$"	$40^1/_2$" x $50^1/_2$"	$40^1/_2$" x $70^1/_2$"	$50^1/_2$" x $70^1/_2$", pieced as necessary

Patriotic

Youth Large/Adult Medium, Finished Size: 40" x 60" (102 cm x 152 cm)
Finished Block Size: 10" x 10" (25 cm x 25 cm)
For information on other blanket sizes, refer to the table on page 31.

SHOPPING LIST

Yardage is based on 43"/44" (109 cm/112 cm) wide fabric with a usable width of 40" (102 cm).

- ☐ 1/4 yd (23 cm) of white solid fabric for blocks
- ☐ 1 yd (91 cm) of blue print fabric for blocks
- ☐ 1/2 yd (46 cm) of red print fabric for blocks
- ☐ 1 3/8 yds (1.3 m) of red/white/blue print fabric for alternating blocks
- ☐ 1 7/8 yds (1.7 m) of fabric for backing
- ☐ plastic poly pellets (see **Step 9**, page 30)
- ☐ size 10 (70) sewing machine needle and size 14 (90) denim sewing machine needle
- ☐ walking foot
- ☐ wrapping paper tube
- ☐ kitchen funnel
- ☐ measuring cup
- ☐ water-soluble fabric marking pen

Cutting The Pieces

*Follow **Rotary Cutting**, page 4, to cut fabric. Cut all strips from the selvage-to-selvage width of the fabric. All measurements include 1/4" seam allowances.*

From white solid fabric:

- Cut 2 strips 3 3/8" wide. From these strips, cut 12 **small squares** 3 3/8" x 3 3/8".

From blue print fabric:

- Cut 5 strips 3 3/8" wide. From these strips, cut 48 **small squares** 3 3/8" x 3 3/8".
- Cut 3 strips 4 3/8" wide. From these strips, cut 24 **medium squares** 4 3/8" x 4 3/8".

From red print fabric:

- Cut 3 strips 4 3/8" wide. From these strips, cut 24 **medium squares** 4 3/8" x 4 3/8".

From red/white/blue print fabric:

- Cut 4 strips 10 1/2" wide. From these strips, cut 12 **large squares** 10 1/2" x 10 1/2".

From fabric for backing:

- Cut **backing** 40 1/2" x 60 1/2".

Assembling The Blanket

Read pages 2-7 before beginning your blanket. Use $^1/_4$" seam allowances throughout.

1. Draw a diagonal line on wrong side of each red print **medium square**. With right sides together, place 1 red print medium square on top of 1 blue print **medium square**. Stitch seam $^1/_4$" from each side of drawn line **(Fig. 1)**.

Fig. 1

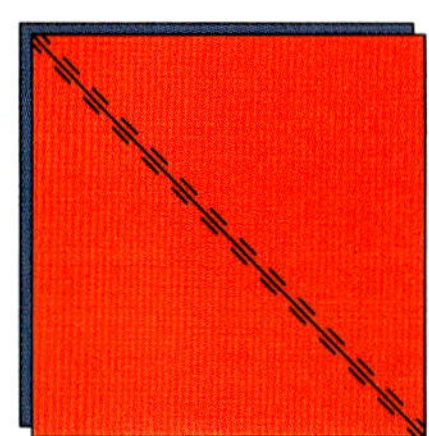

2. Cut along drawn line and press seam allowances toward darker fabric to make 2 **Triangle-Squares**. Make a total of 48 Triangle-Squares. Trim each Triangle-Square to $3^7/_8$" x $3^7/_8$".

Triangle-Square (make 48)

3. Sew 2 blue print **small squares** and 1 Triangle-Square together to make **Unit 1**. Make 24 Unit 1's.

Unit 1 (make 24)

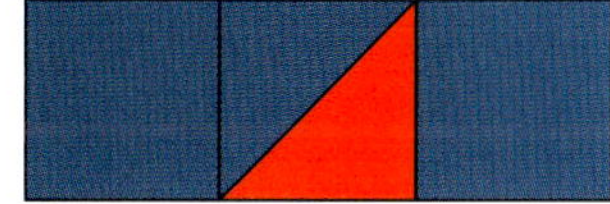

4. Sew 2 Triangle-Squares and 1 white solid **small square** together to make **Unit 2**. Make 12 Unit 2's.

Unit 2 (make 12)

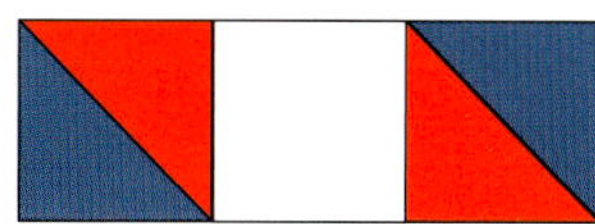

5. Sew 2 Unit 1's and 1 Unit 2 together to make a **Block**. Make 12 Blocks.

Block (make 12)

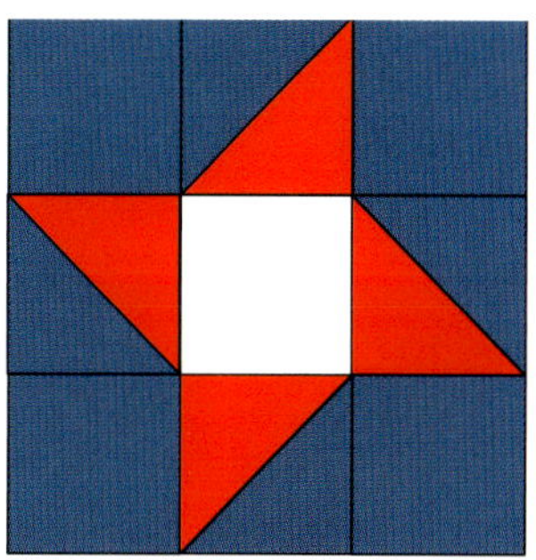

6. Sew 2 large squares and 2 Blocks together to make **Row 1**. Make 3 Row 1's. Press seam allowances in one direction.

Row 1 (make 3)

7. Sew 2 Blocks and 2 **large squares** together to make **Row 2**. Make 3 Row 2's. Press seam allowances in the opposite direction.

Row 2 (make 3)

8. Alternating Rows and direction of seam allowances, sew Row 1's and 2's together to make **Blanket Top**. Press seam allowances toward the bottom of the blanket top.

9. Refer to **Determining the Blanket Weight**, page 3, to determine the quantity of pellets needed for the blanket and how much to place in each pouch. This blanket has 216 pouches.

10. *Refer to* ***Assembling the Blanket****, pages 6-7, to assemble, fill, and close the blanket.* After sewing blanket top to backing, mark the vertical and horizontal stitching lines (shown in red) on the blanket top **(Fig. 2)**. Stitch vertically between each block, along each vertical seam of each Block, and across the large squares vertically where marked to make 12 vertical channels. Place determined amount of pellets in each channel. Stitch in the ditch horizontally between each block, along each horizontal seam of each block, and across the large squares horizontally where marked as you fill the channels to make 18 horizontal channels. Close the blanket.

Blanket Top

Fig. 2

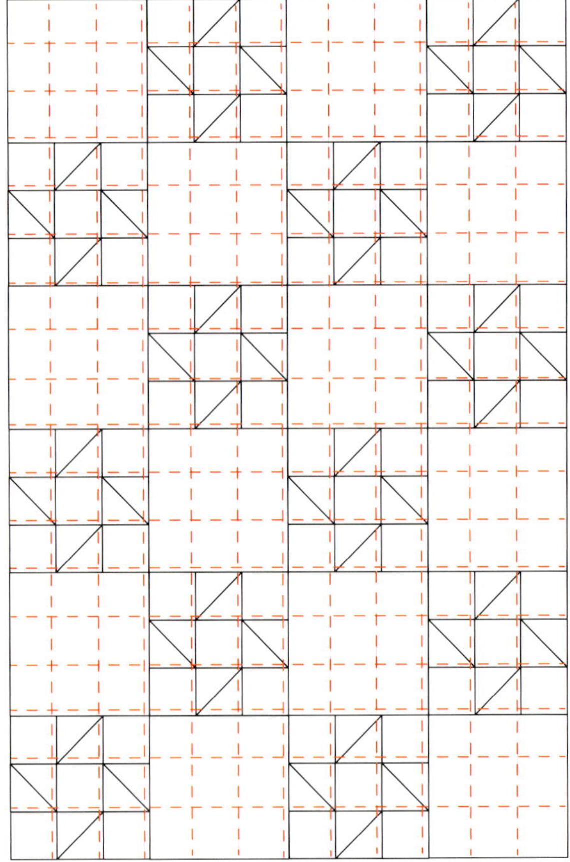

The following table provides the information necessary to make your blanket in other sizes.

	Youth Small	Youth Medium or Adult Small	Adult Large	Adult X-Large
Finished Size	40" x 40"	40" x 50"	40" x 80"	50" x 80"
Fabric Requirements	1/8 yd (11 cm) of white solid fabric 5/8 yd (57 cm) of blue print fabric 3/8 yd (34 cm) of red print fabric 1 yd (91 cm) of red/white/blue print fabric 1 1/4 yds (1.1 m) of fabric for backing	1/8 yd (11 cm) of white solid fabric 7/8 yd (80 cm) of blue print fabric 1/2 yd (46 cm) of red print fabric 1 3/8 yds (1.3 m) of red/white/blue print fabric 1 5/8 yds (1.5 m) of fabric for backing	1/4 yd (23 cm) of white solid fabric 1 1/4 yds (1.1 m) of blue print fabric 5/8 yd (57 cm) of red print fabric 2 yds (1.8 m) of red/white/blue print fabric 2 3/8 yds (2.2 m) of fabric for backing	1/4 yd (23 cm) of white solid fabric 1 1/2 yds (1.4 m) of blue print fabric 3/4 yd (69 cm) of red print fabric 2 1/4 yds (2.1 m) of red/white/blue print fabric 4 3/4 yds (4.3 m) of fabric for backing
Number of Blocks	16	20	32	40
Block Set	4 x 4	4 x 5	4 x 8	5 x 8
Pellet Pouches	144	180	288	360
White Solid Fabric	8 small squares 3 3/8" x 3 3/8"	10 small squares 3 3/8" x 3 3/8"	16 small squares 3 3/8" x 3 3/8"	20 small squares 3 3/8" x 3 3/8"
Blue Print Fabric	32 small squares 3 3/8" x 3 3/8" 16 medium squares 4 3/8" x 4 3/8"	40 small squares 3 3/8" x 3 3/8" 20 medium squares 4 3/8" x 4 3/8"	64 small squares 3 3/8" x 3 3/8" 32 medium squares 4 3/8" x 4 3/8"	80 small squares 3 3/8" x 3 3/8" 40 medium squares 4 3/8" x 4 3/8"
Red Print Fabric	16 medium squares 4 3/8" x 4 3/8"	20 medium squares 4 3/8" x 4 3/8"	32 medium squares 4 3/8" x 4 3/8"	40 medium squares 4 3/8" x 4 3/8"
Red/White/Blue Print Fabric	8 large squares 10 1/2" x 10 1/2"	10 large squares 10 1/2" x 10 1/2"	16 large squares 10 1/2" x 10 1/2"	20 large squares 10 1/2" x 10 1/2"
Fabric for Backing	40 1/2" x 40 1/2"	40 1/2" x 50 1/2"	40 1/2" x 80 1/2"	50 1/2" x 80 1/2", pieced as necessary

Lap Blanket

Finished Size: 18" x 30" (46 cm x 76 cm)
Finished Block Size: 10" x 10" (25 cm x 25 cm)

SHOPPING LIST

Yardage is based on 43"/44" (109 cm/112 cm) wide fabric with a usable width of 40" (102 cm).

- ☐ 1/4 yd (23 cm) of yellow print fabric
- ☐ 1/4 yd (23 cm) of green print fabric
- ☐ 1/4 yd (23 cm) of blue print fabric
- ☐ 1/2 yd (46 cm) of black solid fabric
- ☐ 5/8 yd (57 cm) of black flannel fabric for backing
- ☐ 4 lbs (1814 grams) of plastic poly pellets
- ☐ walking foot
- ☐ size 10 (70) sewing machine needle and size 14 (90) denim sewing machine needle
- ☐ wrapping paper tube
- ☐ kitchen funnel
- ☐ measuring cup

Cutting The Pieces

*Follow **Rotary Cutting**, page 4, to cut fabric. Cut all strips from the selvage-to-selvage width of the fabric. All measurements include 1/4" seam allowances.*

From yellow print fabric:

- Cut 1 strip 6" wide. From this strip, cut 2 **squares** 6" x 6".

From green print fabric:

- Cut 1 strip 6" wide. From this strip, cut 2 **squares** 6" x 6".

From blue print fabric:

- Cut 1 strip 6" wide. From this strip, cut 2 **squares** 6" x 6".

From black solid fabric:

- Cut 1 strip 6" wide. From this strip, cut 6 **squares** 6" x 6".
- Cut 2 **borders** 4 1/2" x 30 1/2".

From black flannel fabric:

- Cut **backing** 18 1/2" x 30 1/2".

Assembling The Lap Blanket Top

Read pages 2-7 before beginning your blanket. Use 1/4" seam allowances throughout.

1. Draw a diagonal line on wrong side of each bright-colored **square**. With right sides together, place 1 bright-colored square on top of 1 black square. Stitch seam 1/4" from each side of drawn line (**Fig. 1**).

Fig. 1

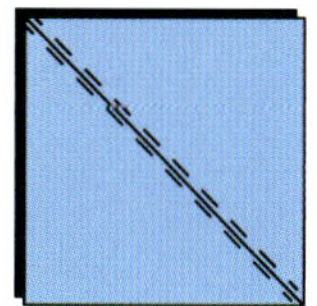

2. Cut along drawn line and press seam allowances toward darker fabric to make 2 **Triangle-Squares**. Make a total of 12 Triangle-Squares (4 of each color). Trim each Triangle-Square to 5 1/2" x 5 1/2".

Triangle-Square (make 12)

3. Sew 4 matching Triangle-Squares together to make a Pinwheel Block. Make 3 Pinwheel Blocks.

Pinwheel Block (make 3)

4. Sew Pinwheel Blocks together. Press seam allowances in one direction.

5. Sew 1 border to each long edge to make **Lap Blanket Top**. Top should measure 18 1/2" x 30 1/2".

6. *Refer to **Assembling the Blanket**, pages 6-7 to assemble, fill, and close the lap blanket.* After sewing lap blanket top to backing, stitch along each seam between the border and the Pinwheel Blocks and through the center of the Pinwheel Blocks to make 4 long channels. Aligning the line with each seam in each pieced Block, mark stitching lines across each border.

7. Place 1/2 cup of pellets in each channel. Let them fall all the way to the bottom. Stitch through the center of the Pinwheel Blocks as you fill the channels to make 6 channels. This will create 24 pouches. Close the lap blanket.

Lap Blanket Top

Neck Wrap

Finished Size: 8" x 36" (20 cm x 91 cm)
Finished Block Size: 3" x 3" (8 cm x 8 cm)

SHOPPING LIST

Yardage is based on 43"/44" (109 cm/112 cm) wide fabric with a usable width of 40" (102 cm).

- ☐ 1/4 yd (23 cm) of yellow print fabric
- ☐ 1/4 yd (23 cm) of green print fabric
- ☐ 1/4 yd (23 cm) of blue print fabric
- ☐ 1/4 yd (23 cm) of purple print fabric
- ☐ 3/8 yd (34 cm) of black solid fabric
- ☐ 3/8 yd (34 cm) of black flannel fabric for backing
- ☐ 3 lbs (1361 grams) of plastic poly pellets
- ☐ size 10 (70) sewing machine needle and size 14 (90) denim sewing machine needle
- ☐ walking foot
- ☐ wrapping paper tube
- ☐ kitchen funnel
- ☐ measuring cup

Cutting The Pieces

Follow ***Rotary Cutting****, page 4, to cut fabric. Cut all strips from the selvage-to-selvage width of the fabric. All measurements include 1/4" seam allowances.*

From yellow print fabric:

- Cut 1 strip 4" wide. From this strip, cut 3 **squares** 4" x 4".

From green print fabric:

- Cut 1 strip 4" wide. From this strip, cut 3 **squares** 4" x 4".

From blue print fabric:

- Cut 1 strip 4" wide. From this strip, cut 3 **squares** 4" x 4".

From purple print fabric:

- Cut 1 strip 4" wide. From this strip, cut 3 **squares** 4" x 4".

From black solid fabric:

- Cut 2 strips 4" wide. From these strips, cut 12 **squares** 4" x 4".
- Cut 2 **borders** 1 1/2" x 36 1/2".

From black flannel fabric:

- Cut **backing** 8 1/2" x 36 1/2".

Assembling The Neck Wrap

Read pages 2-7 before beginning your blanket. Use 1/4" seam allowances throughout.

1. Draw a diagonal line on wrong side of each bright-colored **square**. With right sides together, place 1 bright-colored square on top of 1 black square. Stitch seam 1/4" from each side of drawn line (**Fig. 1**).

Fig. 1

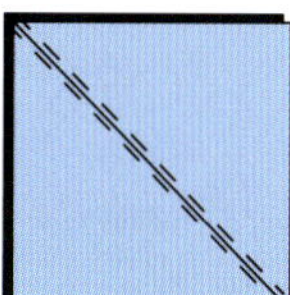

2. Cut along drawn line and press seam allowances toward darker fabric to make 2 **Triangle-Squares.** Make a total of 24 Triangle-Squares (6 of each color). Trim each Triangle-Square to $3^1/_2$" x $3^1/_2$".

Triangle-Square (make 24)

3. Sew 2 matching Triangle-Squares together to make a Flying Geese. Repeat with all triangles to make a total of 12 Flying Geese (3 of each color).

4. Sew Flying Geese together along long edges to make neck wrap center. Press seam allowances in one direction.

5. Sew 1 border to each long edge to make **Neck Wrap Top**. Top should measure $8^1/_2$" x $36^1/_2$".

6. *Refer to* ***Assembling the Blanket****, pages 6-7, to assemble, fill, and close the neck wrap.* After sewing neck wrap top to backing, stitch through the center of the Flying Geese to make 2 long channels. Aligning the line with each seam between each Flying Geese, mark stitching lines across each border.

7. Place $^1/_3$ cup of pellets in each vertical channel. Let them fall all the way to the bottom. Stitch in the ditch between each Flying Geese and across marked borders as you fill the channels to make 12 channels. This will create 24 pouches. Close the blanket.

Neck Wrap Top

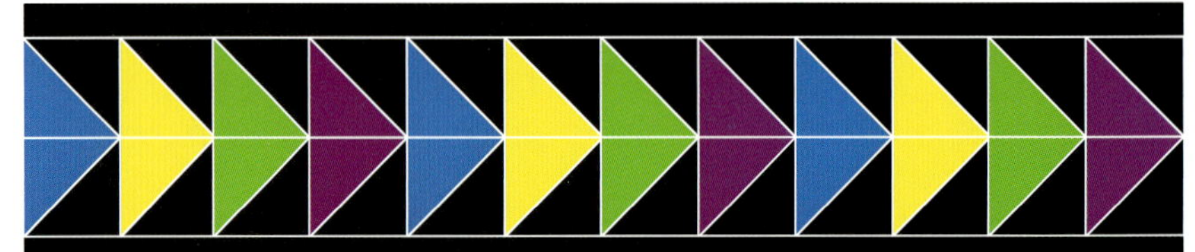

We would like to thank Fabric Editions, Inc. for supplying some of the fabrics used in our blankets.

We would also like to thank Nelwyn Gray and Delorse Richards for sewing some of our blankets.

Production Team: Designer – Kelly Reider; Technical Editor – Lisa Lancaster; Technical Assistant – Mary Sullivan Hutcheson; Editorial Writer – Susan Frantz Wiles; Senior Graphic Artist - Lora Puls; Associate Graphic Artist - Kytanna McFarlin; Photographer - Jason Masters; Photography Stylist – Stephanie Moore.